This Book Belongs To:

____

BY
Home Planners And
Journals
To help you organize your life

* 9 7 8 1 7 9 6 5 9 3 2 0 4 *